First Published in 2017

Published by Master Group

MPC Color, Inc., 5115 East Highland Drive, Jonesboro, AR 72401, U.S.A.

www.mymastergroup.com

Cover Design by Master Group

Illustrations by Amanda Bailey

BELIEVE
TEACH
HEAL
INSPIRE

Matthew Knight is available for keynote speaking, workshops, organization events

and presentations. Please contact mattknightremarkablelife@gmail.com

TALES AND LESSONS

A PLACE TO START...

Marty Sullivan is the newly appointed Director of the Administrative Office of the Courts in Arkansas. He is the fresh father of a beautiful little girl. His wife is gorgeous and as sweet and smart as she is good looking.

He runs marathons. Knows everything there is to know about baseball and has the memorabilia to prove it. He's collected a huge library of classic albums (the round wax kind) across generations of music.

He talks and moves cool, without pretense.

"Genuine" seems like a good word with a big dose of "presence" in the mix.

"Level headed" my daddy would have said.

He is real smart and has a bunch of degrees to prove it.

He treats people gentle and kind and fair. When I have met others who know him, they have nothing but good to say. He is my friend.

He introduced me to TED Talks and I am wiser for it and slightly addicted.

He is why there finally is a book called "Leaving Fingerprints."

It only took him six years to get me to do it. He's become the voice of all the people who would ask if I had a book, as I traveled around the country speaking.

Over those years, I would agree to "get to work on it" but other things...

Then he strongly suggested a deadline and I agreed.

I tried to dictate it. I tried to type it...no mojo.

So, one morning I sat down with pen and paper and began. There was a book in me!

I would take the very rough drafts to Annette Hufstedler who is one of my best buds at Mid-South Health Systems. She is southern sweetness, the mom and grandmother most wish they had. Kind to the core. She typed every single word and asked for nothing in return, 'just to be a part of it.' "Thank you" doesn't get close, my dear.

Susan Ishmael and I go way back. We don't date ourselves with exact numbers anymore when we talk about "way back." Better to say we have sweet history. We have journeyed well together, weathered, tried and true. One of those beautiful people who weave their way in and out of our lives, leave us deeply better. In my tapestry she is gold thread and she is loved for it.

She owns, with her family, Master Print Group. They have won more national awards than they can display, and Susan is the creative force behind it all.

"Susan, here is my book. What do we do now?" And she knew. From the cover to the last page the design is hers. Publishing; promotion...I am in the best hands. Another adventure to share, my truest friend.

Now if you have a book I discovered you need a website and a Facebook page at least. (I need hiking boots for this new learning curve.)

So, Susan brings in a friend, a vivacious little bundle of energy and creative smarts. "Cute as a bug's ear," we would say in the older South. Fallon, is that not a cool name!!! And she is...In no time she knocked out a beautiful website and Facebook page. When people who do what I do see it there will be serious envy drool on their computer screens.

My job now will be making the most of it. I want to do you both proud.

Cheryl is my wife. She is a rare treasure. One of those people who know themselves and their path. Smart, perceptive, can see clear through, but gentle when she offers it.

She loves animals, dogs especially. (We have two, Jacob and Falcon.) She is the kindest person I know. It takes much to love someone like me, but she has and I am ever in her debt of grace. We have traveled much, played in oceans, hiked glaciers, explored canyons, weathered blizzards, and danced in streets.

She will soon have her doctorate in social work. Were we in England, I would be called her consort, having the lesser degree. But maybe that's what I've been all along. Thank you, Cheryl, for this crazy wonderful life.

Mid-South Health Systems has been my work family for 20 years. I started as a therapist (thanks for opening the door, Bonnie White and Frankie Hogue).

Three years in, this remarkable woman, Jayni Blackburn, pulled me into her department, Education and Public Relations. She taught me the way of it – community mental health – and gave me a podium to be its spokesman. She is passed now. It happened right after she retired. But she crammed so much life into every day, motivating and inspiring others – a true life force. You'll find her fingerprints across two decades of my life.

I'm sure other writers experience the same dilemma. We want to express our gratitude to those who journey with us, regularly inspire us. Our fear is leaving someone off our list. But, I figure it's worth the risk and I'm pretty good at apologies. Besides I have stuff for a second book. So, in no particular order, here we go...

Teresa Wilson - joy and grace come to life

Monika Pone - author, confidant, friend indeed

Robbie Cline - to dare the face of God

Asad Khan - beautiful mischievous seeker

Kim Boyette - who can see wonder

Lori Poston - balance in fluid motion

Heather Baxter - wings spread

Derek Spiegel - such adventures shared

Angelina Spiegel - my sister soul

Haydn Huckabee - courageous true heart

Marquisha Applewhite - My partner in crime, the best associate I could ever hope for: we do mental health real good

A Southern Approach:
I would suggest slow reading this book. Do it lazy like a late summer afternoon on the porch. Sweet tea for sure sitting on the table beside you.

(Or a glass of wine by an autumn fire.)

Take it a story or poem at a time. I think there are a couple of dozen of these. And if something speaks to you do something about it.

Any author of similar offerings would like to believe their words could make a reader's life better. And I do also. Another step toward a remarkable life.

Now let's talk about God. I believe in an open system of faith in which God has permission to mess with me. And He has, plenty, as you will see in the stories that follow.

I am convinced that God's love is wild and raging and passionate as is His grace and forgiveness and healing. Stopped by nothing. Our part is saying "yes" and jumping in the adventure. What an adventure it is!

Matthew Knight

leaving
fingerprints

TALES & LESSONS LEARNED FROM A
(SO FAR) REMARKABLE LIFE

ORPHAN

The 70's had bloomed in full regalia.

My brother and I had recently returned from our latest adventure…this one in Nashville…our stab at becoming professional song writers. Unfortunately, several hundred people had stolen our idea at the same time.

Money ran out and home we came to Arkansas. We had cleverly reasoned that returning to Jonesboro was better than the two of us living out of our car.

We were local celebs for at least our "15 minutes of fame"… we may have squeezed 20. Back a month, we were deciding our next attempt at notoriety. When an invite arrived to do a concert at a youth weekend in Louisville, Kentucky, we jumped on it.

About 800 junior and senior high students had shown up for the event. The concert was our best to date…standing O, a curtain call. (We added "rock stars" to our "possible next career list") Actually, there was no curtain. The crowd just clapped a lot, so we sang another song.

Along with the concert, we were part of the team leading break-out discussion groups after each speaker. My teammate was the beautiful (and beguiling) Rosa

Christenson. Our group of 12 well-behaved senior highs were ready to talk. We settled on the lawn outside the conference center and got down to the business of our scripted discussion questions.

Warm up question night one: If you could have something for your life right now, what would it be?

Came to the last guy – John, 17, a senior from a Louisville High School. His answer was about to change my life forever. "What I want is a day with my parents. I am an orphan."

Silence. Pause. Deep breath. Hearts turn. "When I was three, my parents and I were in a car accident near here. They were both killed. No relatives anyone could find. So the orphanage offered to take me. There's a bus load of us from there at the conference."

Tears start and ripple through the group. "It's okay. Don't feel sorry for me. The people at the orphanage have been great. It's just…well…I wish my parents could know me now"…24 eyes worth of tears.

Rosa's hand found mine. "Matt," she half whispered, "maybe we"…"could be his mom and dad this weekend," I finished. We looked to John. "That would be so cool"…deal sealed.

Now Rosa and I were equipped with little more than parental examples and our observations of TV families. I have a friend who uses the quote, "even a blind squirrel finds a nut now and then." In this case, Rosa and I felt like the blind squirrel hoping we could pull this off.

With beautiful expectations, the three of us threw ourselves into it. Breakfast, lunch and dinner, conference speakers, activities, he was between us. In every way we could think we told him how wonderful he was. We even snuck him off campus that afternoon (blatantly breaking one of the big conference rules – oh well). We found a mall and dug quarters out of Rosa's car to purchase a t-shirt for him.

Night two warm up question: What do you want to become in your life?

Answers came, more serious this time. John's vulnerability had refocused the group and, sporting his new t-shirt, it was John's turn. All eyes. "I want to be a good person," he started, "treat people with kindness…try to help when I can.

"My dream…. a surgeon. To be able to give some parents back to their kids. I want those kids to have what I've had today." More tears, group hugs…(at this point, Rosa and I were considering marriage and adoption).

John was smart. 4.0. Full scholarship, honors classes, valedictorian…an innocent confidence, hopeful resolve. His dream appeared to have a good chance.

Sunday morning. A conference center parking lot full of goodbyes. Promises to stay connected, hugs and, yes, tears.

John was on the orphanage bus talking to Rosa and me out a side window. This was turning into a hard goodbye. Our weekend family was disappearing. I was sending a child (John) off to college and saying goodbye to a new "bride" (Rosa) - both about to move across the country on the same day.

For some reason, I had a piece of pad paper and a Sharpie in my hand. Rosa, said, "We need to write him a note."

So we wrote: Dear John, where ever you go, know that there are two people who believe in you and your dreams. Our love, Matt and Rosa.

Before we finished writing, the bus began to roll and I had to run beside it to hand John the note through his window. The last we saw of John was a smiling face reading the gift of our words.

Life folds in on itself. Years pass and memories of even the best of our experiences find their place on the shelves of the mind's library. With the right prompts, we take a volume down and recall its story and sometimes its emotion. But my far-from-static life stays crammed with the immediate and the restlessness for a new adventure. So, John, and for the most part, Rosa, had joined the library.

Twenty-five years later...the Phoenix Airport

My flight out of Phoenix was disappointedly delayed. So I sought solace in the arms of the airport Starbucks (a beautiful child in the cradle of current "modern civilization"). Others it appeared were seeking the same comfort. The line was out the door.

Side Note: My philosophy of Arkansas civilization: When your town gets a Sonic – hope springs eternal; a McDonald's - big change a comin; but a Starbucks – we have moved into the 21st century, trading overalls for skinny jeans, baby.

An unexpected tap on the shoulder broke my prayer that all the blueberry muffins would not be sold. I turned, a man I guessed not much into his 40's was smiling inquisitively. "Are you Matt Knight?"

I'll admit I have had sketchy moments of integrity in my life. I have wondered if grace and mercy would continue to trump Karma. Thought bubble 1: I hope this isn't about one of your girlfriends who I turned to the dark side. Thought bubble 2: the IRS found a problem with that '89 tax return. Thought bubble 3: when their award patrol didn't find me at home, Publishers Clearing House had tracked me here. Let's go with 3. "I am Matt Knight."

His smile broadened. "I've been looking for you for 25 years at least. Do you know who I am?" (now I'm thinking I should have gone with thought bubble 1). "No, I guess not."

"Maybe this will help." He retrieved his billfold. Out of it he carefully freed a tattered piece of paper, unfolding it tenderly for me to read.

D ear John, wherever you go…"Oh, John," I said, "Oh, John." Hugs and tears - the Starbucks line parting, stepping back giving the hugging crying men all the room they needed.

"I knew I would find you or Rosa one day. If I said 'I did it' would you know what I meant?"

"You're a doctor aren't you?"

"I am. Do you remember my dream?"

"I do, giving kids their moms and dads back."

"Yeah! Just seemed right for you or Rosa to know I did it. But this is what I wanted to tell you most of all.

"I breezed through college and was accepted to med school. That first year was so hard, I had to dig for everything, barely slept. By May I had decided I wasn't cut out for medicine after all. I remember packing up all my stuff, sitting on the bed, taking stock, so discouraged, not sure what I would do, where I would go. I opened my billfold to count my meager fortune and out fell the note. I had forgotten it was there. Unfolded, read. Something shifted, settled! Hope. If there were two people who believed in me, then maybe I could do this. I canceled my withdrawal with the registrar, unpacked.

"I taped the note to my study carrel. Every time I was feeling overwhelmed, I would read it and pray. Obviously, that worked.

"I wanted to find one of you and say thanks. I've carried the note all these years. Somehow, I knew it would happen and here you are. Matt…thank you. If you should see Rosa…"

An announcement overhead cut his words short…"That's me, my flight, better run." Quick hug. He was gone.

I have come to believe that events like these are not a coincidence. They are more holy interruptions, dividing mind and spirit, divine insight, gifts from God.

If one enters heaven on good deeds, I'm in. The scene: St. Pete at the gate. My turn. He reads my information with a "this is really sketchy…scowl…really sketchy."

"Wait a minute, Pete. I have three words for you - John, Phoenix Airport."

"Oh, you're *that* guy. Sure, come on in."

Dear John,
Wherever you
go, know that
there are two
people who believe
in your dreams.

Our love
Matt & Rosa

How powerful our words can be. In this case, 22 of them penned by a failing Sharpie on a sheet from a hotel note pad.

Think of words that have shaped your life. Words that inspired, comforted, empowered…words that encouraged, clarified, entertained, thanked, believed…words that healed. And think of the givers of these words, even those that had no idea of their impact on your life.

If you have never said "thank you" please call, write, email… and tell them what they meant to you. You might consider making a list of these heroes. Take your time remembering and recording the ways you have been impacted by their words and the grace they carried. Some of these will be a single encounter (like John). Others could be spread over a lifetime.

Other words took different courses, some, no doubt, destructive. I am not discounting these or their givers, but these will be for another time. Set them aside for now.

And what about your words. In any moment you can choose the words you offer to another person. Another list could be helpful. A list of the people who share your life every day. What words could you offer them. Then do it. The act costs you nothing. (Okay, if you buy a card and then there's your internet bill and the cost of the device you use to send the message…still a bargain.) And then there's the good ole fashioned handwritten letter.

CHRIS

My brother died – a heart attack – several years ago. I miss him every day. Funeral done. Mourners scattered. I was cleaning out his closets and drawers. Sorting the keeps and donates – amazing the amount of stuff we accumulate over a lifetime. Perplexing the meaning some items could possibly have had that saved them from trash. A random set of keys. Two dead watches. A Christmas ornament. I would never know their value treasured and attached to a single life.

The last drawer started out with a couple of sweaters. Then, four brown envelopes and two notebooks. One envelope bore my name. I broke the seal and extracted four handwritten pages torn from a legal pad, dated a year earlier.

In the letter Chris had written, he described what I had meant to him. Across our lives, beautiful words ripping a hole in the grief I had been holding. I sat on the bedroom floor and wept. And in that moment, the very words that brought tears began to bring healing.

His letter is treasure. I read it each January, the month I found it. The words fill me with comfort and resolve to live a remarkable life.

GARBAGE DUMP

Guatemala is a beautiful, wild country and the people reflect that untamed beauty. Travel a few miles outside one of the cities and things become quickly more primitive. Paved roads (rarity)…quickly turning to jeep trails until even the jeep trails disappear. I loved it.

I was there on a mission trip, staying in a compound. A ministry that offered medical service and education, as well as faith.

On my third day after morning devotions, my team leader pulled me aside. We would be going to the market to buy food that afternoon. I would need my passport and some money. Of course, I reasoned, a compound with a hundred staff and visitors had to eat - time to do my share.

The outdoor market in Queseltanango was amazing. Fruits and vegetables, meat and fish, flies and other winged varmints - wouldn't come close to naming half of its offerings.

Those that could in our gathering party were each toting two bags full of the fruits and veggies. Home again, home again… so why were we turning right, not left – not that I didn't trust my new colleagues, but in strange new places, I like to have a vague idea, at least, of my general whereabouts.

"Where are we going," I asked.

"Oh, you'll see," came the replay laced with inside smiles and glances across the van.

"Oh, I get it," I thought. "The new guy's initiation into the Guatemala Scoobie-Doo gang. But I'll admit the further we drove and the more sketchy the neighborhoods became, the more fertile my suspicious imagination grew - too many movies and spy novels in my brain's library. WWJBD...What Would Jason Bourne Do? "

I was starting to formulate a vague escape plan when we slowed and turned into the city dump. We parked on the edge of the landfill near the road.

Then the trucks began arriving. One after another garbage trucks backed up in a jagged row – at least a couple of dozen.

"Won't be long now, Matt. You'll see why we came. Didn't want to spoil it. Hard to believe anyway. Get your sacks." And with that, we stepped out of the van.

Several things happened at the same time. The dump began to move - people out of the rubbage making their way across the broken ground toward the trucks.

The trucks began to dump.

Part of the crowd climbing, falling, digging their way into the garbage. Tossing anything that still looked edible back to their waiting friends. Clothes and shoes that could still be used. Wood, tin, plastic for the shelters.

"Over 5,000 people live here," my team leader whispered. I had seen poverty but nothing like this. I watched and wept.

A tug on the leg of my shorts. Beautiful dark eyes staring up at me. A golden brown cherub five-year-old face. She pointed to the sacks I was holding and then to herself. In that instant, some intense bond was formed.

"Of course they are yours, darling." She waves me to come with her - something I know is against the guidelines of my group.

Guidelines While in Guatemala :
1. Never go anywhere alone
2. Never go anywhere unfamiliar
3. Never go anywhere with someone you do not know

I was about to break some rules. I followed the little girl down the edge of the dump for about 30 yards before I was spotted and we turned left into a cluster of several crude shelters.

"Matt, you can't do that. You need to come back to the van. Matt..."

I pretended I didn't hear. A 10x12 burrow dug into a berm. The opening was lined with rocks and covered with a roof of tin and plastic. Her mother sat in front, nursing a fire with a small black kettle suspended over it. The girl pointed to me, the sacks. The mother was on her feet flinging herself around me. I do not understand her words but her gratitude is plain and I return her hug.

Feelings of falling short take me. I wish I had brought more. Could there ever be enough in this place.

Her father appears, climbing out of their hole and her brother.

He speaks English. Our conversation is brief. My handlers are calling with a sharper tone. He was a teacher at the university for years - ousted when the government changed and put one of its supporters in his place.

I explain I have to go. He says, "We must bless you first."

The family gather around me. He prays. I cry. "Father, thank you for your many blessings. The shelter you give my family... the love we have for one another, bringing a man all the way from America to bring us food for today. May he always know the love of family, may he always have a home and food to eat and clothes to wear. My family blesses him and asks you to bless him, God."

My heart breaks.

Isn't this backwards. I'm the one with everything. They have nothing. No. They had something deeper and truer than me. Forged in fires of suffering. Risen in beauty and strength. I am undone. This is why I came to this beautiful and untamed country…not to bring food but to find my life again. How far off course I had drifted.

Back at the van I was reprimanded. No harshness, only a deep concern for my safety on their watch. I understood. But I would have risked immediate deportation for what I had experienced with this family on the dump.

Eventually, I came home. I saw it all with new eyes. My 1400 square foot cottage was a mansion… my Toyota a Mercedes in the shadow of where I had been. So much stuff. A house full and an attic full. So much to give away. If I hadn't used it, worn it…in a year; if it had no sentimental or historical value, then it could be given.

This was fun - to travel lighter, to appreciate more deeply the things that remained, the beauty and detail and stories they possessed.

That's when something else began to happen. More stuff started showing up, opportunities for income presented themselves. More to share. Thankfulness and gratitude. The flow…

Gratitude and generosity - they do wonderfully strange things. The more you are thankful for the things you have, the more the things you desire appear. The more you give with a heart of generosity, the more appears for you to give. This is truly a life of adventure and abundance.

A simple question for those of you who have much (how thankful you must be). Do not apologize for your wealth. But do you own the stuff or does it own you? Decide what you need, what is meaningful, what is actually used. The rest can be given. Challenge the ideas that "one day I may need this, I may be able to wear that…" Let it go. Define yourself in love and joy and peace, kindness and compassion not by possessions. What an opportunity to find yourself again.

But what if at this point in your life you feel you have little to share. I assure you that is not true. You still have much to give - your time, your talent, your abilities, your words. This is amazing wealth, the real wealth…you. Many groups in your community are looking for volunteers or you might just start a charitable movement yourself to meet a need in the town where you live. Do something soon. Use your life wisely, travel light, journey well. Make a difference. Leave a legacy that matters.

FATHER'S DAY

Father's Day...
and the families around me in the restaurant
bring memories of my sons now grown to men
living far across Tennessee.
I order and call them.
For the few minutes of our conversation,
musings between father and sons,
I can still hear the voices of young boys
with mouths' full of french fries and catsup
and hands sticky with chocolate milkshakes,
as they take turns reading aloud
their handmade cards
on a long ago Father's Day.

(Seldom now am I ever with my sons on Father's Day.
Sometimes they do not call until they realize they have
missed it. Not purposed neglect...only lives too full of other
things as is mine - I am notorious for late birthday cards. But
I always know when it is Father's Day and I always celebrate
and thank God for the honor of two beautiful children. And
for the memories of stuffed mouths and sticky fingerprints
on the homemade cards.)

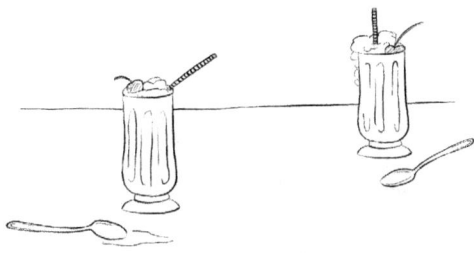

THE MONSTER UNDER THE BED

A Saturday night, the spring of my first year at East Elementary School. Nine P.M. in the bedroom my brother and I shared in a house in Jonesboro, Arkansas's first attempt at suburbs. Living, dining, kitchen, breakfast up front. Bedrooms in the back.

Something wasn't right...

My parents had company over and they were louder than usual. Even with my bedroom door shut, I would hear a word now and then that would have rewarded me a soapy mouth washing. I say this from experience.

I keep waiting for a torte lawsuit TV ad: "If a commercial bath soap was used to clean foul language from your mouth, and, if as a result, you have suffered any of the following diseases------. Please contact the law offices of Johnathan Makerite. You may be entitled to a substantial compensation."

A large fan in the attic pulled air through the open screened windows (air conditioners were just catching on). Thunder was starting to grumble like it was being made to work on a night off. Lightning was low on the horizon, jagged light across the room.

Something wasn't right…

Something was moving under my bed. Scratching. Claws on hardwood. Subtle, but there. Waiting…time for a full out monster alert.

Rules for Engagement for Monster Under the Bed:
1. If a body part is on the bed and covered, the monster under the bed can not touch it.
2. If a body part (even a toe) should slip over the edge, then all of you was fair game for the horror waiting beneath you… even if this was accidentally done while you were sleeping.
3. If possible call for help.

Here's where it got tricky. Some monsters were able to disappear the minute a rescuer entered the room. I know this was true from past encounters with the foul beasts.

By the way, a loving aunt explained those Rules of Engagement to me. Not my cold-hearted, disbelieving parents. "Some of the worse monsters live in Arkansas," she explained. "So fierce they had been driven out of other states." Of course, this could have been a ploy to keep me in bed when I spent the night at her house. But, I wasn't taking chances.

Grrr…so soft and menacing. Gooseflesh!! I positioned myself solidly in the middle of the bed and slipped the covers over my head. How long could I hold out?

AUHUGHR…louder this time. Hungry! This one's not playing around: I'm not moving a muscle, but it knows I'm here. RUGUHHA…time for rule 3.

"Mom, there's something under my bed!!!!!!!!" I say it loudly, not a scream, just a pleaful announcement.

"Go to sleep, Matthew," she yells from the living room. "There is nothing under your bed." Parental laughter from the living room. You would think with witnesses present they would at least pretend to care about my precarious situation.

M inutes pass. The creature is scratching again. Toying with its dinner no doubt. CURHGGH comes the next cry, shaking bed springs!!!!

Loud enough to hear it all the way to the front of the house. "Mom, there really is something under my bed."

"Matthew, we have been through this before. There is nothing under your bed. Now go to sleep." Ripples of polite exasperation in her voice.

Fine, I think…just wait till morning when you come to my room and my bed is empty. Then you'll believe. And you'll feel so sad, so guilty. "If only we had listened…"

GRHBGH. Now "it" knows help is not coming…
"Mom," I can barely get it out.

Knight Household Rules of Discipline - Page 2, Paragraph 5: Dad weighs in on the third strike.

"Your mother told you to go to sleep. Now that's enough." And then the classic gold parental response, "Don't make me come in there." We were an old school, spanking family. Call it what you will, but it was effective – with me anyway. (Once I even had to cut my own switch from the forsythia bush in our side yard. But that's another story.)

CUURZBHQQW!!

That was it!

"I don't care if you beat me." (That should get their friends in the front room looking askance at one another!) "There is something under my bed. Please help me!!"

My dad's footsteps were heavy. A mission. A lighter set on his heels. No, three lighter sets following in his wake. They were all coming. This could work out in my favor. No spanking if this went right. Too many witnesses.

But what if their friends were spankers. "Yes, we agree, Clyde (my father). The boy does deserve one."

Better punishment than death.
My father goes to his knees beside the bed. "We're settling this once and for all. There are no monsters under your bed."

He did not realize what a potentially dangerous position he was in. I had heard the lurking beast. One swift strike and my mother would be raising two boys on her own.

That's when two things happened…My father threw back the bed skirt and the beast let out a blood curdling, bone-chilling…cry. HRCZQRTROW! My dad crashes back into the desk at the side of my bed, "son of a bitch."

Six feet jump back to the wall across the room. Six eyes wide and riveted on my father. He starts to laugh. "Well, I'll be damn. There is something under here."

Now eight knees are on the floor peering through the dust balls at the creature… five creatures now. A mother cat and her four newborns.

"Isn't that Mrs. Turner's (our neighbor) cat? How did it get in here?" (A mystery we never solved.) We are all laughing.

Much discussion about what to do next. My brother, who had slept through this, put the cap on the evening. Chris was a sleepwalker in his early years. He pops up out of bed, looks around as though he is actually awake and taking all this in.

He walks to the window at the foot of the bed, pulls down his pants, and pees against the screen. Finished, he pulls up his PJ bottoms, gets back in the bed, and goes back to dreamland.

This adventure became part of the Knight family lore, told and retold at gatherings of the clan. Somewhere along the line, the story became an encouragement when we found ourselves in hard spots.

"It's only the cat under the bed, honey," my mother would say when we were afraid or anxious or challenge loomed. What seems so big, so frightening often turns out to be much smaller than our worry and imagination had made it.

In our hindsight of such situations, we may smile at the size of our concern compared to its smaller resolution - the boulder to the stone. How many times I have needlessly fretted over something that resolved itself rather simply (effort and determination noted).

My dad's version of the lesson was more colorful. "It's just that damn cat." My brother and I only needed to say, "the cat." Sometimes Chris would add, "Well, piss on it all!"

I've had some serious concerns in my life (some cats are bigger, meaner than others) and I would guess you have faced some also. Not all of them settled as I had wished, but they settled. (They have called for more than "the house cat" level of encouragement.)

Comfort and understanding, rescue, a plan, grace and mercy. More than one person on the sidelines cheering, old fashioned grit and guts. But here I am, scars and t-shirts from the fray, still standing, moving forward. New confidence in my ability to handle the hard stuff.

F ear in all its forms is a powerful thing. The sense or reality that we do not have the resources or control to conquer the challenge - overwhelmed. Another wonderful reason we need one another and a faith in God. To have a person in our corner with words that won't let us quit.

Please. When you are out of "you," bring in the troops. Ask for them. The clearer perspective of another, speaking into the narrow corner that fear helps us paint for ourselves. Every cat can be conquered.

MOVING TRUER NORTH

Is anticipation sometimes better than its object?
On this day, I will relish them both.
Something in my Spirit is shifting
on the edge of breaking free, letting go, once again
The pebble hits the pond,
and ripples swell to waves.
A chunk of snow slips,
and the avalanche rushes to catch it.
I have no idea
the way this turning will unfold.
But this day, I am six years old
and it is Christmas Eve.

(Written on the occasion of a life pending change,
reinvention of self, a step closer to clarity of soul, one of
many in my life. Once feared now embraced, I gather them
to myself and enjoy what happens next.)

BICYCLE

We lived in a cul-de-sac in a neighborhood of breeders. Pink or blue balloons or a cut-out stork with an announcement for a new family member. Bundles of joy arriving regularly. We had done our part prior to our move to the babyhood, procreation five and six.

Signs lining the streets in said neighborhood announced children at play and the need for cautious driving.

Jordan, my first born, had recently shed the training wheels from his bike and had made the transition rather nicely. Michael, the younger brother, saw no reason his training wheels could not be removed also. After six months, "Let's wait a little longer" was wearing thin. One spring Saturday morning, he climbed on my lap, crawled up under the newspaper I was reading. He put a hand on each of my cheeks and squeezed my face to his: "Daddys need to listen to their little boys," he declares. "Okay, I promise you have my full attention. What's on you mind?"

"Remember how you told us that if we had a dream, you would do everything you could to help us make it come true?" "I do recall that and it is true." "Well, last night I had a dream that I could ride my bicycle without the training wheels. So, now you have to make it come true."

Ah, the murky water of parental ethical dilemmas, the challenge of critical thinking blooming a little too early in one of my children, and I haven't had enough coffee to counter.

"Okay, we will give this a try. If it doesn't work, we'll put the training wheels back on and wait a few months. What about that?"

He's back in the living room ready to ride in under five minutes. Another 10 and we were on the curb loosening bolts. Training wheels gone, practice begins. I hold the seat and jog beside him as he gets the feel of a two wheel ride. Down the two blocks and back, steadier each time. He says he's ready.

Hand on the seat, we begin to move. Then the letting go. Just opening my hand and off he flies. (How many times will the hands of my heart open, watching him flying into the places of his life? Each time, taking something of me with him.)

Boy and machine in a flawless journey down the street. I was sure my cheers were disturbing late Saturday morning sleepers, but I didn't care. What a ride he was having and I could see our plan dissolving with each turn of the pedal.

The plan, two blocks down and stop, I join him and get him started again, two blocks back. But…we were obviously past that. The glance back over his shoulder with an "I've got this, dad," smile. He was going for the turn.

Now, turning on two wheels is different than turning on four. Turning had not been part of our prep. That's when it happened…boy and machine falling, sliding across the asphalt into the curb. I'm covering two blocks in Olympic time.

I grab the bicycle that had come to rest on top of my baby, toss it on the grass. Eyes stare up at me, "Daddy, Daddy is my bicycle hurt?" "Michael, we can get a new bicycle, are you hurt?" "Oh yes." I could see the scrapes starting to bleed.

Michael reaches up his arms using words that have defined my life in many ways. "Daddy, gather me." Such a powerful word "gather." Not "pick me up." "Not hold me." Both those, but more. An exchange perhaps in "gather." Comfort for pain, safety for fear, understanding for confusion…

I scooped him off the street. His legs around my waist, his face buried in the crook of my shoulder. I could feel it coming, the quiver, the deep sigh, the tears falling on my neck. A holy frozen moment.

Crying quiets and I start to put him down. "Oh, no, Daddy gather me more." So we stand in the grass beside the broken bike in the spring morning breeze. Quiet. Comfort for pain. Time falls, until he whispers, "I want to go home."

How long do we need to be gathered? Until it's time to go home. How simple.

We arrive and he's fast on the phone to his Gram (grandmother). Does she need to come see him? Oh, yes. Does she need to bring ice cream? Oh, yes. She arrives. He is covered in a box worth of Flintstone Bandaids (most are decorative only). He's milking this. Thinks he may need a toy later when he "feels like going to the store." She agrees. They sit side by side on the couch, gathered, eating ice cream.

In your life, who are, who have been, your gatherers? Those who have comforted, inspired, encouraged, protected, offered affirmation, direction...perhaps to list their names and note the ways they have touched your life. Do you know what they have done for you? Have you told them, thanked them? If not, it is time. A card, call, a text or email. (Words written in your own hand or spoken in your voice are the most powerful.)

And for whom are you a gatherer? Time to tell them you are only a call away.

FRIEND

First time that I saw you
you were laughing
a laugh so full of life
it spilled right over
and all those people
standing round you
scooped up your words
like they were diamonds
and I was thinking to myself
I'd found a friend

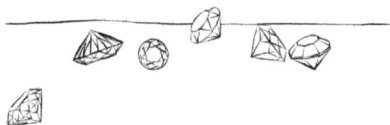

(First verse from a birthday song written for a friend. May you
have a friend whose words are diamonds worth scooping.)

FURNITURE STORE

My sons were running late for lunch. Nothing unusual. So, I had some time to fill. Not difficult in the Green Hills area of Nashville – where the stars shop! I was in the Music City to celebrate Christmas with my boys.

I am drawn to book stores and furniture stores. Reasons that are not for this writing – interesting reasons none-the-less. I wandered into a jewel of a furniture store near Green Hills Mall where contemporary and traditional style had made sweet peace.

Greeting me in the entry was a column, two stories high. Written on its face, ceiling to floor, was the company's mission statement.

I am familiar with mission statements, having carved out a couple for places I've worked. Usually a sentence long with enough words crammed in so it's hard to read in one breath.

But not this one. Thirty-seven beautiful, inspiring, even funny phrases easing their way down from the rafters to the floor. Here are 12 of them:

We are unpredictable
We love to laugh
We don't like mean people very much

We love what we do

We believe in we, not I

We believe in giving great service

We are timeless

We are stopped by nothing

We give to our communities

We never miss a meal, ever

We are curious about everything

Pets love our furniture

These folks knew who they were. I was awed. So simple, so profound.

B ottom of the column, the last sentence – We invite you to join us. Okay. I'm ready. Sign me up. Is this like a furniture club? Do I get cool stuff when I join? Are there special badges or costumes we wear at our meetings? Who do I need to talk to?

As if on some ancient telepathic cue, she appeared. A goddess with lips like Angelina Jolie. An angel of Biblical proportion materializing out of nothing. Those pouty lips were moving, forming sensual, amazing words I was sure. But I was not comprehending all of them. Something about "helping me."

"Thank you," finds its way out of my mouth. "I'm waiting on my sons. Visiting them for Christmas."

"How sweet," she says. Her words drip southern. "Do you like apple pie? We have a little old kitchen in the back." (Lil' ole' kitchen).

"I do."

"Bet I could find some Starbucks to go with that. That be fine, too?"

"Real fine…"

"Then we could look at some furniture together. How about that?" Wait a minute, I think. I must be dead. Hit by a car in the street outside. Because a hot angel just offered me apple pie (my fav) and Starbucks in an incredible furniture store with 37 commandments etched in a stone column. I am in Heaven!

But weren't there only 10 commandments? Moses must have missed a few. After all he was working with two stone tablets, such a small palette.

The goddess takes my arm. She sashays to the back of the store. An up-in-the-club version of "The Hallelujah Chorus" is pulsing in my brain.

Seated across from her at a glass and iron work table, I finished my pie. The vanilla bean ice cream she added left this creamy goop in the bottom of the plate. Something about her made me think about licking it clean. But I resisted the urge.

"So what do you do?" she had asked.

"I'm a therapist – mental health kind."

"Mind if I ask you a more personal question?" She was playing with her top blouse button.

"Not at all." (Yes "personal" – anything you want to know.)

"Well, there's this guy that I've been seeing…" No, no, no. Back to us and sashaying and apple goop and top buttons.

I listened to her tale of woe (and she had one). I offered sage advice in my most compassionate counselor style.

She stares across the table, eyes glistening. "Thank you," she whispers. "So sweet." She touches my hand. "Wish I could find someone like you." Well, look no further! Okay, I may be old enough to be your father, but let's not let something so trivial get in the way.

"I need to walk," she says. "Come with me." We stroll through the store. She's talking about furniture. I'm watching her talk about furniture, touching fabric, trying out chairs.

She starts to apologize for the impromptu counseling session.

"Not very professional."

I stop her. "This happens a lot. People with something they need to tell someone find people like me."

She smiles. I buy a table. I didn't need a table. I had no place to put a table. But it was one of her favorites. She wanted it to be in a home where it was loved. I felt noble, like I was rescuing a puppy from a shelter. "Come home with me little table. I will take care of you. The goddess will be so happy!"

Two guys in the back warehouse wrapped the table and put it in the back seat of my car. At the door, she holds out her arms. The embrace.

"Thank you," she whispers again, "so sweet." and kisses me on the cheek. The door closes behind me. (I'll never wash this cheek again...) What would have happened if I had bought a couch?

The December air hits my lungs...wait a minute. What just happened? I turn. She had disappeared. She was standing at the door seconds ago. She was gone – just like she had first appeared.

In the window I could see the column with its 37 commandments, but the store was empty. And $700 had disappeared from my checking account, a table had appeared in my back seat, and my potential "soulmate" had vanished. Magic was afoot.

The boys are coming up the sidewalk across the street. I cross. We eat pizza. Final hugs and Merry Christmas. I get in the car to head home. I glance back across the street. She's standing in the door. She sees me. She stares beautifully. Her lips move, but I can't tell what she is saying. She slowly raises her hand, touches her lips and opens her palm against the window. She turns.

It's over. Whatever we had, it was done. Perhaps we will both be stronger in the end. (Really Matt, get a grip) I will care for the puppy...I mean table. It will always remind me of you.

Every time I looked in the rearview I saw the table, wrapped in brown packing paper that crinkled when I hit rough spots in the highway – looking less like the puppy that needed a good home.

W hy had I bought it? Okay, she was mesmerizing but... Wait a minute. What started the whole adventure in the furniture brothel? That's it – the greeting column! Up in your face – come on in – here's who we are - you can be part of us.

Identity established.

Could I do a column for me? I never had attempted to write down who I was. I had shared scripts in a bunch of small groups over my life and graduate school assignments. Even produced a flimsy personal mission statement in a training I attended, and done a little journaling. But nothing like this. The big picture of me.

How ironic. A mental health professional who helped people decide who they were, who they could be. And I had never attempted to purposefully take the same journey. Never too late to get started. The longest journey began with a single step, etc…or in this case "word."

I got home, stored the table in my "not sure what to do with this" room. Took every picture off the wall in my hallway and started to write.

I know this is difficult for some of you to read. Your mother told you never to draw on the wall. Maybe you were punished for doing so. I was. But my wonderful mother was dead and not making my house payments.

My wall, my magic marker.

Too much happens in a day to pay attention to it all. Our brain tends to focus on the immediate and disregards the rest. I knew this would take some time and it did. Two years and some change.

When something stood out in my day – a thought, an emotion, an experience, idea, observation, a memory…I made a note

– a word or phrase to remember it later. When I was ready to do "wall time," I would ask this simple question: what does this tell me about myself?

Over time, patterns began to emerge – insight, understanding I had never known. I was liking this clearer picture – more comfortable, more content in my skin. Even the flaws were looking better, becoming manageable. The ghosts of my past - hurt, fear, guilt…were moving on to do their haunting somewhere else.

Of course my friends thought they should help. Some of their offerings were for "mature audiences only," but I let them leave their mark. Some were hilarious. Some were surprises. A serendipitous peek at me through others' eyes. A few were surgical, cutting through my defenses to the truth of me.

I recently painted a wall in my garage with chalk board paint. It is time for me to do this again – an update of this journey into my 60's. A new wall to fill!

I invite you to join us, the "keepers of the columns, the writers on the wall" in an incredible adventure to discover "you." It does take time, but a valuable use of it for sure.

You can write in a personal journal. Use large post-its or flip charts. One person told me she was writing on the walls in her closet, another family is using their formal dining room, a wall for each family member.

I offer over 100 questions to get you started. Contact information is in the introduction. I will send them to you.

Special Note: If along the way you discover things forgotten, painful, powerful…then share these things with a friend or perhaps find a good counselor for a season. You'll be amazed at what can happen.

FIFTH GRADE MUSIC TEACHER

She asks us to close our eyes
and listen to the music.
"What do you see in your imagination?"
The music ends.
Again the question.
No one raises their hand but me.
I saw horses white and black and speckled brown -
running down a mountain.
The rest of the class laughs,
especially the boys.
The recess bell rings.
She is at my desk, her beautiful face close to mine.
"I saw the horses, too," she says.
"We have a special gift,
you and I.
And we won't let what someone says
take it away from us.
Will we, Matthew?"
"No ma'am," I say.
And she hugged me tight.
And I never did.

(She was a practice teacher from Arkansas State College.
One of the people who changed my life forever with her
wonder-filled words. That 11 year old boy still whispers to
me, grown to the plus side of sixty, and clings to the gift she
gave to his heart that spring afternoon.)

MANTRAS

"What do you want, Matt." Read these words again with a tone of challenge and sarcasm. Monika is being my therapist (and a damn good one) in my face, direct. Dr. Phil wishes he could be her. No doubt I was whining about something of "great importance" (again with sarcasm).

"You don't even know what you want."

"Yes I do," I snap. "To win the lottery and achieve world peace."

She rolls her eyes. "I ask a serious question and what do you do. Of course, you detach and make a joke - so predictable."

"Sometimes, maybe, but not all the time," weakly defensive. "I'll have a list next time of everything I want and I'll read real slow and it will be real long and you'll have to listen to every word." I sound like I'm eight.

And the banter continued until next subject.

At pivotal times in my life when I am asked a question, I may in that moment not realize how important the question is. But eventually something about it lodges in my brain and demands an answer.

"What do you want, Matt?" The pursuit of this particular answer opened a treasure of understanding that continues to direct my life today. The power of my intention, my belief, filling my world with abundance and the experience of God's grace – amazing!!

For two years I wrote and rewrote. I could say I wanted a new car and that was fine. But what did having that new car mean? Was there something below the vehicle that was the truer desire? More here to learn than just a list of wishes. I was discovering myself. Sometimes frustrating, sometimes epiphany, worth every minute of both.

So, I ask you the same question posed to me. "What do you want?"

Following is my mantra, my confession of my expectation, my intent for the day, my prayer... my answer to Monika's question. It is a living, changing document. The statements describe events that happen in my life every day. And this works for anyone willing to take this journey.

These examples are a few of my more general intentions. There are more personal ones that are not here. But enough for you to get an idea for a list of your own.

This is one of the best days of my life.

I love and am loved.

More wonderful experiences and people than I can imagine
find me and I them.

I look for the best in each person I meet.

I laugh often and deeply.

I listen.

I am grateful and thankful.

God's incredible protection surrounds me,
my family, and my property.

I find meaningful places to share my resources and abilities.

I take time to be still and breathe.

I have opportunities to learn new things and
refresh things I have always known.

I pay attention to the lessons and insight that life brings to me.

I have health, healing and rejuvenation physically,
psychologically, and spiritually.

I have wealth and abundance and share it
generously and live simply.

I see my work not as a task but as an opportunity
to share my gifts and abilities.

I see my flaws, admit them openly
and find forgiveness, healing and change.

I forgive those who I believe have wronged me.

I eat a healthy diet and exercise regularly.

I have stamina, energy, and ability for a full life.

I choose and maintain healthy, positive relationships.

I will have the knowledge, wisdom, and creativity
to make the decisions and complete the tasks before me.

I will accomplish the things that are necessary and with
peace let the rest wait their turn.

My sons have opportunity, favor, success,
prosperity, and health throughout their lives.

The company I work for expands and prospers and is the
provider of choice in every county we serve, attracting and
keeping the best employees to meet the needs of our clients.

These things that I have declared most loving God,
with a thankful heart, I allow to overtake me.

As you develop your list here are some things to remember:

1. Research has regularly shown that goals written down and repeatedly spoken are 70-80% more likely to happen.

2. Take your time. Read through your list out loud. Pause with each statement. Picture what you are declaring. Ask… how will I feel when this happens?

3. Part of your brain may fight you at first…"This is stupid, naïve" it will say. To this part of your brain say… "I hear what you are saying, but I am doing it anyway, so be quiet." You may need to use stronger language. After a while much of that resistance will stop.

4. In a real sense you are brain washing yourself - forming neural pathways that are positive and expectant.

5. When things begin to happen (and they will) please be grateful and thankful and willing to share.

6. If you share this process, some people who are from-the-womb negative will offer their criticism. Disregard this. In the end your results will speak for themselves.

7. "What do you think you deserve?" One of my friends who practices this quite successfully asked me once…"Would you rather be the guy who needed a car or the guy who could give one away?" I upped my expectations and have been able to do just that.

8. What a joy to be detached from "stuff," able to give freely, having much to give. This is pure joy.

9. Does everything you write down happen? Most of it, if you consistently commit yourself. As for the rest…not yet, just wait! This is a process. It takes time to develop but is well worth every minute. You may even change your mind over time - that is fine. Adjust the list and move on.

10. For those of you who are faith based folks this should work very well with your prayer life.

If you should hit a snag in this process please do not hesitate to contact me. My information is in the front of the book.

WEDDING

And the pages turn
in the book of your days
and their beauty burns brighter
as they yellow and gray
even in ending
may they always beg
beg for the words of your love

10,000 DAYS

(The refrain from 10,000 days, written for my son's
wedding, never performed. But even as it takes its place
with the songs I play for myself on quiet nights, it is still one
of my best wishes for their life together. I love you both so
much, Michael and Ashley.)

ONE GOOD DEED

She is living next door at her aunt's house. Taken in by my incredible, compassionate neighbor recently retired from Arkansas State University.

Barely in her 20's with a suitcase of bad decisions. The move initiated by an abusive spouse. With her, a child who will die soon from severe physical deficiencies. Some would have quit, just stopped moving or stepped away. But she is a fighter – a waitress at a Wings Sports Bar - minimum wage plus tips.

A mother devoted to a child - thankful for one more day. They share a room decorated with walls full of art and photos celebrating what will be their brief life together.

On this day, she is in the driveway scraping off her windshield. She is determined, but so is the ice. Her breath the color of the sky threatening more snow.

I am pulling into my garage when I see her. My car is warm. I can smell supper when I step out, but it will have to wait. Another thought turning to purpose –

One Good Deed…

I found the book "One Good Deed" by Erin McHugh. I thought it was lost. During the end of this year's organizing and donating, there it was - the author's account of 365 days of good deeds.

For three years I have journaled each day things for which I am thankful and grateful.

(New Epiphany! Positivity Alert!) What if I included a good deed done each day in my journal?

Thankfulness has now become something spontaneous throughout my days. So much to be thankful for. There is a chapter in this book dedicated to this practice.

So what if I purposed a good deed? Where would this go? A page was turning inside me. This was right.

I started January first. In my journal, I now record a good deed each day. Already, I am aware of a shift. What will I do this day?

And as I look for the one, I see more than one. Many opportunities to act positively. What we give our attention to, really does get bigger.

…And there she is in 13 degrees of winter twilight. No gloves, last of the day's light waning. Scraping…scraping, trying to get to work, where she will do a different kind of scraping. The tragic fighter next door. I walk across the yard, my scraper in hand.

"Let me help you."

She looks up – strange mix of surprise and appreciation. "Please…"

I suggest she start her car. Her car - worn with a handicap lift on the back. Perhaps running by her sheer determination. The heat inside the Ford begins to make our job easier.

"Hope your work goes well tonight," I say.

"Thank you so much."

"You are courageous."

She's not sure what to say…"Thank you."

I wonder if very many people speak positively to her.

I turn to supper and warmth.

In my journal – helped the woman next door scrape her windshield.

In my heart – I am changed…

I recently shared this idea with a work colleague. She asked if making dinner, especially when she didn't feel like it, could count.

I said, "Sure, maybe even as two good deeds."

The next day, she said she was thinking as she cooked, " 'This is my good deed today.' I was surprised how different I felt from my last meal prep."

She added that her good deed tomorrow will be getting two kids up, dressed, fed, and to school by herself. She hopes it has the same results.

I invite you to join the movement – one good deed a day.

ALASKA TOUR BUS

Lisa Cassidy is a wood artist
story teller
preservationist
dog lover
and Sunday tour guide in Alaska

and from her heart
she reflects the pristine beauty
of this wilderness

caught up
in the wonder of the moment
I decided to ask her to marry me
but my wife was on the bus
so I didn't

(An uncommon life...Lisa was celebrating the arrival of her
Toyota Forerunner that morning. It had taken three months
to get there and she would need it badly come winter.)

POT ROAST AND PREJUDICE

My dad was prejudice, born of prejudice in 1914.

Black people were "niggers." They were rowdy children who needed a firm hand. He was a Klansman – more concerned with control (they needed to stay in their place) than hatred and terror.

At six, I had no idea what this meant. What I did have was healthy curiosity. One morning in October I was rummaging through my parents' chest in their bedroom looking for my father's sword. He was a 32nd Degree Mason, whatever that was. But you got to wear a real sword, so it must be good.

Instead I found what appeared to be a ghost costume. A sheet with cool eye holes and a pointy head. Halloween was just around the corner. Would he let me use this treasure to trick or treat? Did my father go trick or treating? Maybe he wore it to "grown up" Halloween parties. Whatever...I needed to try it on.

Okay, it was a little long, but that's what safety pins were for. My mother was in the kitchen. Matt Knight, aka Casper the Friendly Ghost (some of you will have to google Casper), was about to pay her an unexpected visit.

With too much "happy" in my voice, I crept into the kitchen.

"Booo, booo! Momma, it's Casper the Friendly Ghost. Umm," She was preoccupied? "Momma, it's Casper," I persisted.

She turned, screamed and began yanking the costume off me. She was muttering something about telling dad to "burn this thing," She was mad, I mean mad. And she was cursing, which she hardly ever did. "Get this off of you."

I thought I was about to get it - a spanking, confined to my room all day, bread and water. Then, getting it all over again when my dad got home. It was just Casper??? Well, I'd not be watching those cartoons again…fast learner, Matt Knight.

When she calmed down, she apologized, even cried a little. I was dodging punishment – Woo, Hoo!!! She explained that my father had belonged to a club that wasn't very nice. He wasn't part of it anymore. The costume I found was like a uniform they wore at their meetings.

"Don't mention this to your father – our secret. When he gets home, I'll take care of it." Sworn to secrecy. This was getting better by the second. But if secrecy meant my freedom…so be it!

Looking back I wish I had been the proverbial "fly on the wall" to observe this particular exchange between my parents. Later, in my teen years, I brought the incident up over dinner. My mother gave me the eye, then gave my dad an even more threatening eye, and declared, "I don't know what you're talking about."

By then I knew the truth – the Casper costume had been my father's Klan robe, and I was being raised in and taking on the prejudice of my father.

Aunt Grace: Grace Matthews was one of my mother's three sisters. She never married. Instead, she gave her life to living and learning. Barely five feet tall, she would fearlessly strike out to see the country (usually by train) and bring back tales of her adventures to her students. And although I never sat in her classroom, I was her favorite pupil. And though she was loved by the people of Crossett, Arkansas, where she spent most of her years teaching 5th grade, I loved her more.

She planted in me this beautiful wanderlust, not just to go to a place, but experience it, find its secrets, contemplate its meaning, wonder at its beauty.

"It's one thing to know about something," she would say. "It's another to truly understand it." She could turn a dirt clod into a life lesson.

I was 10. My father had been upset right before he went to work one summer morning. A "nigger" that owed him money "better have it today."

My aunt was having coffee with mom who was about to

leave for the beauty shop. She saw and heard his anger that morning as she had many times. When they were gone, she sat me beside her.

"Come here, Cly Jun (short for Clyde Junior). I have some things to tell you. Your father is a good man. He works so hard. He provides food and clothing and a home for you. He loves you, even if he has trouble showing it sometimes. But we all have some things we are wrong about. Your father is wrong about black people."

So much of who I am is because of who she was. An epiphany at 10. I knew she was right. On that summer morning, a social consciousness was born in me. She talked to me about slavery, the worth of every person, the beauty of our differences.

For the next three years, she took me with her on her summer adventures, showing me a world I would never have seen in the city limits of Jonesboro, Arkansas - people and cultures so different than mine, cities and deserts, lakes and oceans, any shade of person you could imagine. The beauty of it was overwhelming.

And she warned me about confronting the prejudice of my father. "It is so deep in him," she explained, "generations deep. You cannot change him. He will only fight you if you challenge him."

I should have taken her advice. Many verbal barrages ignited the air of our den. The civil rights movement was in full swing and in the TV news most nights. Scenes of protest and response – peace and brutality.

I thought Dr. King was so brave. My father saw him as an "uppity nigger" who someone should put in his place. "Someone needs to kill that bastard and his NAACP cronies."

Then I was angry and shouting about equality and…most nights the battlefield was bloody with no victor. I finally would just leave the room, but God did not.

Church: I was in college at Arkansas State University, a senior close to graduation. My parents were concerned about my faith. Church had become an option not often taken. Usually my visits to First United Methodist on Main Street in Jonesboro involved bribery.

"If you'll go to church with us today/tonight you can stay for lunch/dinner (usually pot roast or fried chicken)." My mother was a fantastic Southern cook and she often sweetened the deal with a homemade cake or pie that could make the back-slidden say "Amen."

In my defense (and let's start with the bottom line), I knew I was going to heaven. And I still loved the huge marble edifice where I was baby baptized and pre-teen confirmed, Sunday school, youth groups, boy scouts, a dozen mentors – I was there for it all! I thought of my current collegiate condition as more of a hiatus, extended vacation. In my heart, I knew I'd be back, sooner or later, on a more regular basis.

*Note: I left Jonesboro in my 20's – lived in several places, traveled many other places, did a variety of work. Eventually, I returned to the town of my birth and attended First United Methodist Church (FUMC) on Main Street. I have come home. My parents (in heaven) no doubt have breathed a sigh of relief as they await our reunion. However, I have no plans for said reunion to happen any time soon!

A spring Sunday night (with the promise of pot roast and coconut cream pie at the after party). I was sitting in the middle section of the main sanctuary three from the end. Seat one on the aisle contained my father.

Besides the food, my mother said I was in for a "a special treat" for the evening gathering. A youth singing group from First Church Pine Bluff would have the entire service – including guitars and original music. I was feeling glad I was there.

Time came, pastor's intro, and out came the groups of junior and senior highs, singing as they filled the altar area. Holy ba gee gee! A third of the group was black!

I turned to see my father. This was going to be great! If he had an orifice that wasn't puckered or a vein that wasn't pulsing I'd 'a been flabbergasted!...My mother instinctively put her hand on his arm, prepared to grab him if he moved. I just grinned.

Churches in Jonesboro were segregated in 1969. I could not remember seeing a black person in the church building. Even the custodians were white.

Not only were these young rapscallions in the church, they were at the altar. And beautiful did they sing! About every other song one of the youth would share a testimony telling what God had done or was doing in his/her life. I teared up more than once, while my father appeared to be on the edge of cardiac arrest.

Charley came to the microphone. Average looking black male, 16 years old, and then he sang. Pin drop silence. God was there. My mother was sniffling now, along with most of the church. With one hand she rummaged in her purse for a Kleenex, the other still on my father's arm.

Charley finished but didn't leave the mic - his turn to speak. "I was raised to hate white people. My father went to prison for a while. Some white people he worked with accused him of a crime that had been committed on a job site. White accusers, white judge, white jury. They found out later he was innocent and he was released.

"Never trust a white person," he would say. "Never think that they are your friends, even if they seem nice. They will do you wrong at the drop of a hat, always put themselves first. To them, you just a no good nigger! All my life since I was little, over and over. It must be true. He was my daddy.

"But God found me. (I was so angry). Then these guys found me. And God melted all that hate and replaced it with love. This is my friend, Jack." A white teen came out of the group, looped his arm over Charley's shoulder. We wrote the last song together. It's a song about love and forgiveness, a chance to start over."

And then it happened…

My father lunged into the aisle and headed for the altar. My mother's heroic efforts to get him back included an arm-grab-attempt-in-the-side-lean-position. Her Olympic form failed.

This was getting better by the minute. My mother muttered something about bail money. By then my father was standing in front of Charley and Jack. "Oh God, please forgive me. I've been so wrong," as he crumpled to the carpet.

The mic was on. We could hear snippets. "Young man, pray for me. So tired of this hate."

Charley and Jack were on their knees beside my father. They were praying. Then the whole group was there, surrounding my dad. Praying and singing "Amazing Grace". They helped my father to his feet. White and black arms embracing him. The church on its feet applauding. (In those days FUMC was a formal, proper church in which such displays of emotion were infrequent.)

Silence on the way home. My dad took some sweet ice tea and went to sit in the backyard. My mother and I ate pot roast and pie. We quietly discussed the miracle we had seen. "Let him bring it up," she said. Good advice, which this time I took. He never did.

Instead, I never heard the word "nigger" again. He never missed church. He started hugging my brother and me, even saying he loved us (hardly ever did before this happened). He fixed up his rental property that housed black tenants. He laughed more and would ask to do things with my brother and me. Grace had come to Clyde Louis Knight. He was not the same. God had healed his hurt, lifted his anger - to be vulnerable again, to know love without fear.

I think about that night still - my father falling at the altar and grace and forgiveness, a chance to start over - Jack and Charley's song and prayers. Sooner or later we are all there. At an altar in a church, or a car, or a bedroom... "please forgive me; I've been so wrong." Seeking to be reconciled to self or others or God, seeking love that reaches past our flaws and finds our hearts. The embrace, the presence, the release.

And there are those who need our forgiveness. We will be wronged. You learned this lesson in grade school. You can hold the offense until it turns to rancid bitterness or you can let it go. You may need some help with this, especially if it is old and deep and mean! But I assure it can be done and it is worth the process. The weight of it gone.

In either case, your freedom. You have a choice.

BICYCLING ACROSS AMERICA

I am traveling in a series of "theres" he says
What are "theres" I ask
I get to a place and then I'm "there"
So I rest, replenish my supplies, note what has
happened so far…
Then I start peddling again

How many "theres" are in your journey I ask

He smiled… enough for a lifetime

The next week I bought a bike

(I met him at a wedding in Arizona. He bicycled into Phoenix
just in time for a friend's nuptials. He was traveling from
California to New Orleans. After that he wasn't sure. He was
the only one at the reception in bicycling attire.)

THE FAIR

I watch children cling to cheap toys
won from midway hucksters with toothless smiles
won by parents, money running thin
heading for the parking lot and hard won freedom from the
sensory overload
of this year's county fair.
I watch a strollered paraplegic girl with eyes roving just this
side of oblivion.
She takes more delight in the plastic streamers,
rainbow colors hanging from the ceiling rafters,
dancing under air conditioning vents.
The crowds passing her glance pity, then divert their eyes
as if looking away would make her imperfections disappear.
I decide she has the better idea
and sitting behind my booth,
I look up to watch the rainbow dance above.

(Even the simple are sometimes wiser. I think of her every
year when I man our company's booth at the fair. I always
look up wishing they still hung streamers. And I bless her for
her gift to me that night.)

BASEBALLS AND BALLOONS

Michael, my youngest, was six. We were into baseball bats, balls, gloves, hats, t-shirts. "We" being Michael, the older brother, Jordon, and me, the financier of two little boys' diamond dreams.

And let's not forget the cards – smiling faces of the rookie and pro, the famous and the want-to-be famous and the once famous. All waiting in shiny packages, along with something that favored bubble gum crushed and fattened to a 2X3 inch square. Squares packed with sugar that could keep two brothers awake well after bedtime discussing stats, flashlights under the covers arranging their cardboard treasure in proper order. Squares that teased the promise of their favorite player just waiting below the slick wrapper.

I had promised Michael some catch and batting practice on a Saturday afternoon. For six, he had an arm and accuracy. Pop – the ball repeatedly hit my glove in the hot June air. Pauses only to chase down the throws that went high or wide.

We were about to break out the bat, when I received a phone call. I needed to return to work, unusual for a Saturday. But "it wouldn't take long," maybe half a hour. With any luck, I would be there and back, round trip and meeting, in an hour or so.

Michael was not sympathetic – baseball far outweighed work. Obviously I needed to get my priorities straight.

"You promised, Daddy." Are many of us who are parents not haunted at times by the unkept promises we make and break? And usually for good reasons. But reasons that meant little to our children and often became only disappointment in the beautiful eyes that stared at us and our explanations.

The meeting – a promotion and a $10,000 (slap-yo-mama-and-break-into-your-happy dance) raise. They wanted to be sure I'd say "yes" before they announced it the next week. Boy, did we ever need the cash! "Of course I'll accept – thank you so much. I'll make you proud." My mind was shifting back to baseball when…

My "this-will-only-take-30 minutes" meeting was well into its second hour when God intervened. The pregnant secretary across from me suddenly screams, "my water is breaking." In no time she was on her way to the delivery room and I was on my way home.

Michael was waiting on the front porch, baseball gear in a pile beside him. "I'm mad at you, Daddy. You said one hour and it's a lot longer than that." "I'm so sorry, Michael. The meeting was a lot longer than they said it would be. But, baby boy, daddy got a $10,000 raise and a promotion."

Unimpressed. "But you said we could practice batting." "We will just as soon as I tell your mom." Mom was impressed. After an hour of pitching and catching and chasing balls, along with several reprimands on tardiness, we were showered and were ready to celebrate.

I n my guilt, and exuberance to celebrate our good fortune, I had let the boys choose the restaurant. What was I thinking – not the dreaded Show Biz Pizza!! A pizza joint built for kids, filled with enough electronic gaming to drain a parent's pockets and patience dry. And if the dinging, whizzing, beeping machines and screaming children weren't enough…while you ate marginal pizza, you were serenaded by life size plastic animated animals playing instruments, singing and cracking jokes. But the boys loved it and I threw myself into it because they did – very convincingly, I might add.

It had been a good day! And along with many other memorable good days that have filled my life, it took its place in the storage files of my mind.

The dream: I awake crying. The baseball, the meeting, the raise, even Show Biz – I've dreamt it all. Out of storage into my sleeping consciousness, bringing with it a unique sadness. But why? What a wonderful mystery to solve – a few days of blindly missing the obvious.

One thing did occur to me later that day as more details of the actual event surfaced. It had been colander night at Show Biz. If a family would wear colanders on their heads while ordering on certain nights, they would get their pizza for half price. The things we do for our children, bordering on buffoonery, and even years later their glee still ringing in our ears.

The Epiphany: A few days after the dream, I was watching a father herd his two boys through Target to the checkout counter. "Oh, Dad, look at this…can we please have that…" Their adventure brought back memories and empathy for the harried father. In that moment, something fell back inside me and I knew. What would I give to have a day with my sons at that age again. $10,000? Of course, and there it was – the mystery of my dream unraveled.

The residual guilt I had accumulated over the years choosing other things over the most important people in my life. I always gave them shelter, they never went hungry, but they had me only in snippets of Saturdays, holidays, and vacations. I had traded the best for the good, so many times.

I headed for the Target door, choking back the tears, barely making it to the car before the flood. The memories played through like a harsh film with a remorseful sound track. I was undone. Prayer. In the end, I decided to talk with my sons. I had sins of omission that needed confession, recognition, and perhaps forgiveness.

Lunch: - Two weeks later, I was in Knoxville with a mission. Michael who was working while he attended the University of Tennessee (UT), had taken a long noon break to take his dad to lunch. At a high-end pizza place, doing my best to hold it together, I tell Michael the story. He didn't remember the baseball disappointment but was impressed by the raise. I tell him I would give it all back to have that afternoon with him again. He smiles.

"I don't know how to ask this Michael. I realize now how much I put other things in front of you and Jordan. I wish I had done it differently. It breaks my heart. I'm sure there were times it broke yours too. Could you ever forgive me?"

He can see the tears - reaches across the table, puts his hand on mine. "Dad, it's not what's behind us that matters. There are always things we could have done better. I forgive you, sure. But I love you and know you love me. It's what's ahead of us that matters now." The greatest gift my son will ever give me.

"Now, let me tell you a story," he says. "It was Ethan's birthday. (The boy's mother had remarried and had a son, Ethan.) I told him he had $25 to spend and thought he would want a toy or video game. Instead, he wanted to go to Jubilation Station, a mini amusement park filled with electronic games, bumper boats, batting cages, go carts...all designed to suck the cash out of parental (and grand parental) pockets. I explained to him that the $25 would go fast. But that's what he wanted. Off to Jubilation Station. Thirty minutes after we hit the entrance, the birthday money was gone. Ethan was not happy. 'Get more money,' he complained. I reminded him that I had said the money would go fast. He was getting more upset. So, I bribed him with a helium balloon to get him out the door. 'Let's tie it to your wrist, so you don't lose it.' I had three bucks in this 10 cent balloon and was trying to protect my investment.

"No, '[he] could hold it!' In the car, I suggested we tie it to the door handle. 'No', again. We headed toward home down the interstate. Two minutes and the balloon was out the window…highway history. Ethan was screaming. Out of his seat belt, on the floor, pounding the seat. 'I want another balloon now.'

"I think I channeled you, Dad. 'Ethan, (in my sternest tone) get up out of that floor, get that seat belt back on, stop that screaming now!' I had never spoken to him that way, It scared both of us. In an instant, he was in his seat belt, wide-eyed, sitting at attention.

" 'Ethan, I didn't mean to scare you, but you had to stop acting that way. You're gonna lose some things. We're not going back to Jubilation Station today. But sooner or later, Ethan, you'll get another balloon.'

"Dad, you and me, we can't go back to that afternoon, but we can always get another balloon."

College was paying off. How wise Michael was becoming. How insightful, articulate. I could see my genetic half percolating away. (Okay, probably his mother's.) But, the truth he spoke was powerful and freeing.

And we have...had many other balloons and adventures and life shared, well lived and loved.

We all have things to let go of. Guilt, fear, sadness, whose memories are uncomfortable, sometimes debilitating. They shape the way we judge and experience our lives, ourselves. They hold us back from going on, from allowing ourselves to experience the best, be the best. But, we can let them go, find healing.

"Do you want to be well?" This is our choice, always our choice.

Most of us will need some help with this. A friend or mentor or therapist or clergy who will listen to our story, who has insight/ wisdom to offer. Someone to see the big picture around our snapshot of dilemma. Whose words point a pathway back to ourselves.

My heart boasts a beautiful scar where the guilt once festered. I visit it again in the telling of this story. It shines with the white lines of love that have replaced it, a life more defined. Gratitude and thanksgiving now for the wounds that brought me here, for the power to heal, for the power to be.

MID NOVEMBER

On this day of high fall
On this day of mid November
when the sky is the blue of your eyes
and the River Birch
by the terrace
bare branches resting
on the edge of winter sleep
leaves offered to the earth again
and the breeze comes
with a colder bite
against my face
on this day of possibilities
of adventures
yet unlived
of turning seasons
I think of you, my love, of you
and the autumns waiting ahead

AUTUMN TURNING

Fall is binding up
the frayed cords of summer
and turns to us
as she ties her bundles
with kisses
of cool nights and sighs
of coral moons

(I am a child of October…spent this November afternoon
watching the sun set until the autumn golden light and long
shadows disappeared. Writing of love true and
beauty deep.)

BEAUTIFUL COINCIDENCE

Two books. One arrived a year earlier than the other as a birthday present - Ann VosCamp's *1000 Gifts*. I read the intro and the first chapter, skimmed through the rest. Looked like a very good read, so it took its place on the table by the bed to wait its eventual turn.

Several months later I was finally reading *1000 Gifts* (with a Kleenex) as part of my morning devotions. Like for so many, her words were cool water for my thirsty spirit.

About halfway through Gifts, the second book found me. It was waiting on a book rack at Kinko's. (Who knew Kinko's sold books?) I was waiting impatiently for copies for a work project.

I had read her first two offerings - Rhonda Byrnes' *The Secret* and *The Power*. They were powerful, inspiring, opening the world of intent and attraction for the first time for many readers.

But, I had no idea there was a third book, *The Magic*. A quick perusing and it was on its way home with me and the copies.

At the same time, I was working on a presentation about Positivity - positive psychology and mindfulness. (I realize this is starting to sound like one of those novels that introduce three random characters whose lives are about to collide leaving them changed forever.)

I have come to believe there are few coincidences. In this case, when three things with the same message arrived at the same time, I should pay attention. And just at a time I needed something new, fresh. That vague discomfort, restlessness with things as they were, seeds of self-reinvention germinating below the surface.

And that is what happened...two books, one presentation - a theme running through them that would become one of the most important practices of my life - purposed thankfulness and gratitude.

So, I began a journal. Every morning (or evening) I write at least three things for which I am thankful, grateful. Over two years and 4000 entries.

Often before I write, I open the journal (which will be filled before this book is published) and read the reminders of the beauty in my life. I can even measure the year based on the remembrance of the blessings I recorded.

Much of my thankfulness never makes the journal. The practice has become spontaneous as I move through my day. All around me is so much to be thankful for, the obvious, the almost hidden.

From my journal:

I am grateful and thankful for...

*Gourmet tacos with my family and friends in Nashville,
Christmas dinner a week early*

A gift of front row seats for a play at the Orpheum in Memphis

The smell of air when the rain is coming

Warm coats on cold days

My expressive dog, Jacob

Half and half in morning coffee

Indoor plumbing

A phone call and good visit with my oldest son

Chimney smoke against a perfect night sky

A few examples of gratitude from yesterday's walk through
my office complex...

*The guys in maintenance that magically
made the artificial Christmas tree fit back in its original box*

A copy machine and color printer

Morning greetings from friends at work

*Annette who has typed (translated) this
manuscript from my difficult penmanship in her spare time*

A great new CEO and department supervisor

Clearing most of the to-do stuff on my desk this week

*The beautiful plants in the business office breezeway
that Sue has nursed back from the brink of death*

This idea of recording thankfulness is suggested across so much of the literature I have researched in positive psychology. Our brains love this, pumping endorphins to match our gratitude, forming neural pathways of positivity affecting thought, emotion, behavior.

The people who practice it (and the number is growing) report the richness it adds to their lives. Give it a try. Any of the books I've mentioned may inspire you to begin. So little time for such a great payoff.

LECTURE HALL

She directs a program at a college where I was speaking. I have known her several years. She is a good person – real good – you know this at first meeting.

But her year had not been so good. Her husband called it quits after 24 years. One of her children came close enough to death to see the tunnel and light. Deep faith and a strong core – she is rising.

She meets me in the parking lot – my official escort to the lecture hall. She is smiling. I return her smile and offer my arms. She presses in. "So good to see you," I say. She is silent. Right away God is near.

"My beautiful friend, I know this has been a hard, hard year for you." Her head nods against my chest.

"I should have done more. I am sorry." Comfort short and overdue. She breaks. The eyes reveal what the heart can't hide. Rich tears.

"I wasn't intending to make you cry."

"These tears are not for the bad year," she whispers.

She pulls back. She wants me to see her say this.

"I just can't remember the last time someone called me beautiful. Thank you, Matthew."

And there it is. Our hunger for someone to see us, validate us. Whisper beauty. Waiting in all of us, sometimes near starvation.

We walk to the hall. Sweet silence…

We long for words, beautiful words, to lodge in our heart. Defining memory and emotion across our lives. Words of grace that the heart deserves. And sometimes, even unintended, we end up giving someone the very gift they need. Ironically, I am writing this on Valentine's Day. What a wonderful opportunity for "beautiful."

BEAUTIFUL

TIDE POOLS

my heart is full of twisted consequence
and blessing deserved and undeserved
people I have loved
losses suffered
gifts shared
guilt noted
grace accepted
beauty and tragedy tethered in dance

my heart is the tide pools on this beach
holding the incredible memories of the sea of my life
temporarily separated from their source
awaiting high tides
reunion
but for now a playground for children building sand castles
….where's my bucket and shovel

ROCK STAR

He was famous - as fame goes among those who do research in mental health – a psychiatric rock star in the treatment of depression. I don't remember his name.

I was attending the annual mental health institute. An August event held in Central Arkansas – an opportunity for professionals in the field to earn some needed continuing education hours.

He was opening the three day show. We sat in a hotel ballroom, anticipation like the minutes before the band appears at a less geek venue. Manna about to fall from psychological heaven, the priest about to offer blessing.

The introducer, president of the counsel, reads from a scripted bio, gushing with the admiration of a groupie. She has practiced this, delivering her lines like the female lead in a high school play. I don't remember her name either. She is breathy like some act of impromptu passion just transpired between her and him in the green room backstage.

Profuse academic applause.

He's across the stage, brief hug with her. She is beaming. Cameras flash. She will no doubt make sure the conference photographer sends that photo to her. Where will it be displayed? On her office desk? Perhaps the wall? Maybe tucked away in her secret bedroom drawer at home.

He takes the podium as he has taken others in other concert …I mean, lecture halls. We sit ready to write – poised legal pads and pens from the conference packet (packets complete with t-shirts and a schedule).

He stands quietly and takes us in, eyes moving slowly over us – a shepherd about to lead his flock to green pastures.

And then it happened…

He turns away from the podium and walks to the back of the stage. He appears to be in deep thought. Ah…he has found us worthy, gathering his best thoughts, only his purest water will do for the waiting thirsty.

A minute passes (which in these situations is a long time). A second minute, he paces a little. Quiet murmurs in the audience. Could he be ill? Is this a test, part of the lecture?

I'm sitting with the cool kids (mid 30's to 50's). We whisper - decide this is about to be a clever illustration. Wait for it, wait for it…

Or…what if we were weighed and found unworthy, lacking. Maybe he has just remembered that Arkansas is the 48th ranking state in education. Is he at the back of the stage dumbing this down for us?

Then he turns. Back to the podium. Pin drop silence.

"When you can tell me the purpose of your life in three words. And you are true to living these three words. And you don't allow yourself to be distracted from this course in your life… you will be happier and more successful. You will be healthier, have better relationships, make better choices. Three words …pause…now about depression."

But it was too late. Who cares about depression. I'll buy his book. I have a quest. Three words. My purpose. This is exciting. Should have done this years ago.

I'll just knock this right out. Be done by the time he is. So I wrote.

First word . . .

Father – but wait, that's more a role than a purpose – what does it mean to be a father – the purpose below the role . . . okay, this will take a little longer than I thought.

Let's try another word . . . Christian – okay, I am a Christian but what is the purpose in being a Christian. That's a lot of words…more than three for sure.

Oh, my. This will take some thought . Maybe by the end of the conference I can get this narrowed down.

But in the next two years...I had two. Ten more years... three...and last year, a fourth. Lots of writing, observing, erasing...living.

Believe | Teach | Heal | Inspire

These four weaving their true and holy patterns across my life, even when I did not recognize they were at work.

And the times I didn't heed them – consequences followed for sure. Then purpose remembered, recovery was much easier, the path regained. What a wonderful compass they have offered.

After sharing this and getting responses over the years, I am sure that it does not take others as long to find their three words.

And this would definitely be one of those messages I would share with myself if I could time travel back to visit me at 25. Find your purpose...and, of course, buy Wal-Mart and Apple stock the instant it is offered.

Overall, I have been true to these purposes. And the depression celeb was right. I have been happier, more successful, experienced better relationships...I even get paid to be me. How cool is that?

This is part of who I am and to know my purpose is such

power and peace. I am so grateful and thankful for this understanding, even if it has come a little later in life wearing a few more scars.

Here it comes. How about you? Can you tell me your purpose in three words?

Take your time. Be true to what you have learned. Let me know how your journey goes.

OTHER VOICES

My son, Jordan, is a free spirit. He has paid the price that those who follow other voices often do. But scars barred, he has risen up. Course set on a life extraordinary. He is one of the main reasons I believe it is possible for a broken wanderer to find a truer way. What an inspiration he is to me.

I attended a three day retreat several years ago. Unknown to the participants, friends and family had been asked to write letters passed out on Saturday afternoon. Here is Jordan's epistle to me. True treasure framed in my office. Read often…

When we start this life, dreams and ambitions are hardly considerations. Between then and now are the times for finding a voice; a proving ground. We aren't expected to change the world, only that we piece together the parts that make a difference in the world we know. Along the way are all the distractions we never expect. Many people choose the complacent path, but some are not satisified with simply fading into societies' fabric. Those are the ones who desire not only to live, but to know life. These are the ones called hero.

I never once went hungy. I never went without heat or clothing or shelter. Often my desires were treated as the demands of a king. Because of you I have flourished. I am a person I was not and could not have been without you. I have always been proud of you.

Thanks Dad,

Jordan

HERO

I WILL BE WAITING

On the day of my death let there be singing
Let there be dancing and many a toast
And with glasses held high let each one step forward
And tell of the things they remember the most

So when you gather, I will be with you
You'll find my love in the comfort you share
In the midst of the music listen so closely
And you'll hear my voice along with yours there

Chorus
Sing for the grave and sing for the cradle
And sing for the days that made us all smile
Find sweet surprise in every tomorrow
God's laughter and grace in every mile

On a day in October scatter my ashes
Let them go flying in the sweet autumn wind
When the sun's at the place it turns the earth golden
I'll return to the arms of God once again

In the days of your life follow your heart's song
And let it always be kindness you seek
At the end of the light I will be waiting
With arms open wide and a kiss for your cheek

(If you happen to attend my funeral, you may be surprised at who you hear singing this song. Written especially for the occasion, I hope you will do as this humble composer has asked…even if you have to wait till after you leave the church. And at the end of your days, I will be waiting just past the gates. Please look for me, as I will you.)

AUTHOR

For the last fifteen years, Matthew Knight has worked in education, public relations, and marketing for Mid-South Health Systems, an Arkansas Community Mental Health corporation. He develops and provides a variety of training programs for business, industry, and educational groups as well as Mid-South staff. In addition Matthew handles much of the public relations and marketing in Mid-South's thirteen county area. Prior to his current position, Matthew was director and therapist at Mid-South's Paragould Outpatient Clinic for three years.

As a Licensed Professional Counselor, he has thirty years experience in mental health services. He provides education, consulting, and motivational presentations across the U.S. In his life he has been a junior and senior high public school teacher, the administrator of a private school, started two businesses, written music in Nashville, produced an award winning motion picture, and traveled extensively. His first book, *Leaving Fingerprints*, you are holding in your hands.

Matthew completed his bachelor's degree in education at Arkansas State University, a master's degree in counseling psychology and family studies at the University of Tennessee, and pursued post graduate studies in psychology at ASU.

www.ingramcontent.com/pod-product-compliance
Lightning Source LLC
Chambersburg PA
CBHW060054100426
42742CB00014B/2825